Mealtime
Blessings

Andrews McMeel Publishing
a division of Andrews McMeel Universal
1130 Walnut Street, Kansas City, Missouri 64106

www.andrewsmcmeel.com

ISBN: 978-1-4494-3646-9

Library of Congress Control Number: 2012939915

ATTENTION: SCHOOLS AND BUSINESSES
Andrews McMeel books are available at quantity discounts with bulk purchase for educational, business, or sales promotional use. For information, please e-mail the Andrews McMeel Publishing Special Sales Department: specialsales@amuniversal.com.

Mealtime Blessings

Prayers, Blessings, and Meditations for Saying Grace

Kathleen Blease

Andrews McMeel
PUBLISHING®

Also by Kathleen Blease

The Catholic Mom: Nurturing Your Household

I Can't Wait to Meet My Daddy

Love in Verse: Classic Poems of the Heart

A Friend Is Forever:
Precious Poems that Celebrate the Beauty of Friendship

A Mother's Love: Classic Poems Celebrating the Maternal Heart

Sensual Love Poems

A Book of Joy by Thomas Kinkade (compiled by Kathleen Blease)

Introduction

Ever since man has gathered to break bread, a mealtime prayer has helped to bring family and friends together in a shared understanding: Our bodies have been nourished by God, both physically and spiritually, and we are thankful.

What a wonderful gift we can give to our families at mealtime! Beginning dinner with a remembrance to Our Heavenly Father definitely has a special effect. During a moment of prayer, the house is quiet, work stands still, our hands stop moving, and only words of thanksgiving break the silence. It is peaceful and private and shared with family and others who make up our daily lives. It brings us closer together, united in the quiet moment. Certainly a different speed than what our busy schedules produce.

Mealtime is an opportunity to remember those who are in need, as well. God hears our words and sends comfort to those for whom we pray. Believe me, I personally know the gifts many people have given to my husband, my children, and me through their prayers. (My mother would say it simply: "Prayer works!") In addition, if we are mindful about the nourishment we receive at our table, extending a prayer to others makes us particularly humble and grateful. Unique and edifying, and all in a simple, quiet moment.

Like my other book, *Nighttime Prayers*, this collection has no particular order, rhyme, or reason. It is meant for you to peruse at your leisure, giving you time to read how others of our faithful community raise their voices to Our Heavenly Father. I love reading and reflecting on prayers. It gives me a chance to put myself aside and delve into a new perspective of our omnipotent God.

Remember, a prayer can be fanciful or robust, sounding like a symphony. Or it can be silent and humble, made of only a single thought or word. Lift up our hearts, and God hears all.

May the Lord bless your family and friends as they gather around your table. I once heard a mother call dinner time her "family hug." Yes, even with rambunctious teens at the table, I can certainly say Amen!

Kathleen Blease
Pennsylvania

Mealtime Blessings

Prayers, Blessings,
and Meditations for
Saying Grace

$\mathcal{T}$his is the day of the Lord! Let us
rejoice and be glad in it! Let us thank
the Lord for daily food, health, and
the blessings of our home. Amen.

—Traditional Orthodox Catholic prayer

Our Father, who art in Heaven,
Hallowed be thy name. Thy kingdom
come. Thy will be done on earth as
it is in Heaven. Give us this day our
daily bread, and forgive us our tres-
passes, as we forgive those who tres-
pass against us. And lead us not into
temptation but deliver us from evil.
For the kingdom and the power and
the glory are yours forever. Amen.

—The Lord's Prayer

$\mathcal{L}$ord, behold our family
here assembled.
We thank you for this place in
which we dwell,
For the love that unites us,
For the peace accorded us this day,
For the hope with which we expect
the morrow;
For the health, the work, the food
and the bright skies
That make our lives delightful;
For our friends in all parts of
the earth. Amen.

—Robert Louis Stevenson (1850–1894)

$\mathcal{B}$less us, O Lord, and these thy gifts
which we are about to receive from
thy bounty through Christ,
Our Lord. Amen.

—Traditional Catholic blessing

$\mathcal{D}$ear Lord, thank you for the rain
that feeds the earth. Thank you
for the food that feeds our bodies.
Thank you for your words that feed
our souls. Amen.

—Author unknown

$\mathcal{D}$ear Lord, thank you for this food, your daily gift to our home. Make us joyful for your daily gift and make us attentive of those who are in need. Amen.

—Author unknown

$\mathcal{G}$ive us, O Lord, thankful
  Hearts which never forget
  Your goodness to us.
  Give us, O Lord, grateful
  Hearts, which do not waste
  Time complaining.

—Saint Thomas Aquinas (1225–1274)

We thank You, Lord, Giver of all good things, for these Your gifts and all Your mercies and we bless Your holy name forever. Amen.

—Traditional Orthodox Catholic prayer

$\mathcal{T}$he Lord bless you and keep you!
The Lord let his face shine upon you,
and be gracious to you!
The Lord look upon you kindly and
give you peace!

—Numbers 6:22–26

For health and food,
For love and friends,
For everything
Thy goodness sends,
Father in Heaven,
We thank Thee.

—Author unknown, widely attributed to
Ralph Waldo Emerson (1803–1882)

$\mathcal{C}$ome, Lord Jesus, be our guest,
and let these gifts to us be blessed.
O give thanks unto the Lord for
He is good, and His mercy endures
forever. Amen.

—Traditional Lutheran prayer

Sacris Solemniis

At this our solemn feast
Let holy joys abound,
And from the inmost breast
Let songs of praise resound;
Let ancient rites depart,
And all be new around,
In every act, and voice, and heart.

Remember we that eve,
When, the Last Supper spread,
Christ, as we all believe,
The Lamb, with leavenless bread,
Among His brethren shared,
And thus the Law obeyed,
Of all unto their sire declared.

The typic Lamb consumed,
The legal Feast complete,
The Lord unto the Twelve
His Body gave to eat;
The whole to all, no less
The whole to each did mete
With His own hands, as we confess.

He gave them, weak and frail,
His Flesh, their Food to be;
On them, downcast and sad,
His Blood bestowed He:
And thus to them He spake,

"Receive this Cup from Me,
And all of you of this partake."

So He this Sacrifice
To institute did will,
And charged His priests alone
That office to fulfill:
In them He did confide:
To whom it pertains still
To take, and the rest divide.

Thus Angels' Bread is made
The Living Bread for us today:
The Living Bread from heaven
With figures does away:
O wondrous gift indeed!
The poor and lowly may
Upon their Lord and Master feed.

You, therefore, we implore,
O Godhead, One in Three,
So may You visit us
Who worship You with glee;
And lead us on Your way,
That we at last may see
Where You dwell in Eternal Day.
Amen.

—Saint Thomas Aquinas

$\mathcal{C}$hrist, bread of life,
Come and bless this food. Amen.

—Traditional Lutheran prayer

$\mathcal{D}$ear Father, hear and bless
  Thy beasts and singing birds;
  And guard with tenderness
  Small things that have no words.

—Author unknown

$\mathcal{E}$ach time we eat,
  May we remember God's love.

—Prayer from China

$\mathcal{B}$lessed be thou, Lord God,
  Who bringest forth bread from
      the earth
  And makest glad the hearts of
      thy people.

—Ancient Hebrew prayer

The eyes of all things do look up and
trust in thee; O Lord, thou givest
them their meat in due season, thou
dost open thy hand and fillest
with thy blessing everything living.
Good Lord, bless us and all the goods
which we receive of thy bountiful
liberality; through Jesus Christ our Lord.

—Queen Elizabeth I (1533–1603)

Dear Lord, the eyes of all look hopefully to you, and you give them their food in due season. You open your hand and satisfy the desire of every living thing. You are just in all your ways, and holy in all your works. You are near to all who call upon you. May my mouth speak the praise of the Lord, and may all flesh bless his holy name forever and ever. Amen.

-—From Psalm 145

Mary Star of the sea!
Look on this little place;
Bless the kind fisher race,
Mary Star of the sea!

Send harvest from the deep,
Mary Star of the Sea!

—From "Cadgwith," Lionel Johnson (1867–1902)

So God who gives us daily bread
   A thankful song we raise,
   And pray that he who sends us food
   May fill our hearts with praise.

—Thomas Tallis (c. 1505–1585)

Here a little child I stand,
  Heaving up my either hand;
  Cold as paddocks though they be,
  Here I lift them up to thee,
  For a benison to fall
  On our meat and on our all.

—Robert Herrick (1591–1674)

Savior, bless these Your gifts which
we receive from Your hand. May the
light of your resurrection shine in us
and through us to all, for Your honor
and glory. Amen.

—Traditional Orthodox Catholic prayer

Thou hast given so much to me,
  Give one thing more—
      a grateful heart;
Not thankful when it pleases me,
As if Thy blessings had spare days;
But such a heart whose very pulse
      may be Thy praise.

—George Herbert (1593–1633)

$\mathcal{B}$less us, O Lord, Bless our food and drink, You Who has so dearly redeemed us and has saved us from evil. As You have given us this share of food, may You give us our share of everlasting joy.

—Traditional Irish blessing

$\mathcal{B}$less this food to our use, and make us mindful of the wants of others; for Christ's sake, Amen.

—Author unknown

The Selkirk Grace

Some hae meat, and canna eat,
And some wad eat that want it;
But we hae meat, and we can eat,
And sae the Lord be thankit.

—Robert Burns (1759–1796)

A Grace Before Dinner

O thou, who kindly dost provide
For every creature's want!
We bless thee, God of nature wide,
For all thy goodness lent;
And, if it please thee, heavenly Guide,
May never worse be sent;
But, whether granted or denied,
Lord, bless us with content!
Amen.

—Robert Burns

O Lord who fed the multitudes with five barley loaves, bless what we are about to eat.

—Arabic grace from Egypt

O Lord, let the light of your
countenance shine upon us!
You put gladness in my heart, more
than when grain and wine abound.

—Psalm 4:7–8

Almighty God, who has given us
grace at this time, with one accord
to make our common supplications
unto Thee; and dost promise that
when two or three are gathered
together in thy name, Thou wilt
grant their requests, fulfill now,
O Lord, the desires and petitions
of thy servants, as may be most
expedient for them; granting us in
this world knowledge of thy truth,
and in the world to come life everlasting. Amen.

—Saint John Chrystostom (c. 347–407)

The hungry shall eat and shall
      be satisfied.
Those who seek the Lord shall
      praise Him;
Their hearts shall live forever.
Bless us, Lord, and these Your gifts
Which we are about to receive.
For You are blessed and glorified
Forever. Amen.

—Traditional Orthodox Catholic prayer

May the blessing of the five loaves
and two fish, which God divided
amongst five thousand men, be ours;
and may the King who made the
division put luck back in our food
and in our portion. Amen.

—Traditional Irish blessing

$\mathcal{G}$lory be to the Father, and to
the Son, and to the Holy Spirit.
As it is now and ever shall be.
World without end. Amen.

—Traditional Catholic prayer

Father, we thank Thee for the night,
And for the pleasant morning light,
For rest and food and loving care,
And all that makes the world so fair

Help us to do the things we should,
To be with others kind and good,
In all we do, in work and in play
To grow more loving every day.

—Author unknown

$\mathcal{T}$he poor shall eat and be satisfied,
and those who seek the Lord shall
praise Him; their hearts shall live
forever! Amen.

—Traditional Orthodox Catholic prayer

May our Lord, who changed water into wine, give joy to our hearts, and keep us thankful. Amen.

—Traditional prayer

O great Spirit, whose voice I hear in the winds, and whose breath gives life to all the world, hear me! I am small and weak; I need your strength and wisdom. Let me walk in beauty, and make my eyes ever behold the red and purple sunset. Make my hands respect the things you have made and my ears sharp to hear your voice. Make me wise so that I may understand the things you have taught my people. Let me learn the lessons you have hidden in every leaf and rock. I seek strength, not to be greater than my friend, but to fight my greatest enemy—myself. Make me always ready to come to you with clean hands and straight eyes. So when life fades, as the fading sunset, may my spirit come to you without shame.

—Traditional Native American prayer

The grace of God and the favor of Patrick on all that we see and all that we do. The blessing that God put on the five loaves and two fish, may He put on this food.

—Traditional Irish blessing

$\mathcal{T}$he Lord remembered us in
      our misery,
  God's love endures forever;
  Freed us from our foes,
  God's love endures forever;
  And gives food to all flesh,
  God's love endures forever.
  Praise the God of Heaven,
  God's love endures forever.

—Psalm 135:23–26

$\mathcal{F}$or the joy of human love,
  Brother, sister, parent, child,
  Friends of earth, and friends above,
  For all gentle thoughts and mild,
  Lord of all, to thee we raise
  This our hymn of grateful praise.

  For each perfect gift of thine
  To our race so freely given,
  Graces human and divine,
  Flowers of earth and buds of heaven,
  Lord of all, to thee we raise
  This our hymn of grateful praise.

—Folliott S. Pierpoint (1835–1917)

$\mathcal{L}$ord, bless the food and drink of
Your servants, for You are blessed
always, now and forever. Amen.

—Traditional Orthodox Catholic prayer

A Better Resurrection

I have no wit, no words, no tears;
My heart within me like a stone
Is numbed too much for hopes or fears.
Look right, look left, I dwell alone;
I lift mine yes, but dimmed with grief
No everlasting hills I see.
My life is in the falling leaf;
O Jesus, quicken me.

My life is like a faded leaf,
My harvest dwindled to a husk;
Truly my life is void and brief
And tedious in the barren dusk;
My life is like a frozen thing,
No bud nor greenness can I see;
Yet rise it shall—the sap of Spring;
O Jesus, rise in me.

My life is like a broken bowl,
A broken bowl that cannot hold
One drop of water for my soul
Or cordial in the searching cold;
Cast in the fire the perished thing;
Melt and remold it, till it be
A royal cup for Him, my King;
O Jesus, drink of me.

—Christina Rossetti (1830–1894)

We thank You, Christ our God,
that You have satisfied us with Your
earthly blessings. Amen.

—Traditional Orthodox Catholic prayer

About the Author

Kathleen Blease is a longtime book editor, author, and columnist and a full-time home-schooling mom of two rambunctious teenage boys. After many years in publishing, she started her blog, *Kathleen's Catholic: How Grace Drizzles In*, to encourage other moms raising their children in faith, sharing her homegrown wisdom gleaned during nearly two decades of marriage and motherhood. Kathleen's blog also features *The Little Catholic Kitchen*.

Her columns have also appeared regularly at CatholicMom.com, CatholicExchange.com, and CatholicLane.com. She is also a book reviewer for *The Catholic Company*.

Kathleen lives in the hills of eastern Pennsylvania with her husband and their two sons.

www.ingramcontent.com/pod-product-compliance
Lightning Source LLC
Chambersburg PA
CBHW070802050426
42452CB00012B/2454